Key Stage 3
Level 4 Workbook

Name: _____

Class: _____

Mathematics

Lois
Helyar

Contents

Introduction

This Level 4 Workbook is the first in a series written to support the Letts Key Stage 3 Mathematics Classbook.

The Workbook covers mainly Level 4 material, though some of the ideas are developed a little further than this. Each piece of work is divided into one of three categories, indicated on the Contents page:

- *Exercises* provide an opportunity for further practice and consolidation of material introduced and explained in the Classbook;

- *Activities* also connect to corresponding parts of the Classbook, but tend to be more open-ended and practical in nature;

- *Investigations* enable you to begin to explore a new area of mathematics, using familiar skills in an unusual or novel context.

This Level 4 Workbook is designed to help you move smoothly from primary to secondary school mathematics. Spaces are provided for most of the answers, but an exercise book will still be needed in order to provide space for working. When the book is finished it should be kept safely as it will be a useful source of revision when preparing for Key Stage 3 National Tests (SATs) and end of year examinations.

Most of the work is designed to be done without a calculator. Icons on the title bar of each page indicate this, and links with the Key Stage 3 Mathematics Classbook are clearly shown where appropriate.

The author, Lois Helyar, teaches at the Royal Mathematical School, Christ's Hospital, Horsham.

1 Place value and powers of 10

1.1 Multiplying and dividing by 10 or 100

Solve the following problems without a calculator, using the methods you know for multiplying and dividing by 10 or 100.

1 A crate holds 100 cartons of fruit juice, each containing 750 ml. How much juice does the crate contain in total?

....

2 A market gardener is planting gooseberry bushes in rows of ten. There are 117 bushes altogether. How many rows will there be?

....

3 Julia has decided to put a fence down each side of her garden. Fencing costs £15 per metre, and the garden is 50 m long. How much will it cost her?

....

4 There are 30 chairs in each classroom in the Mathematics Block at Upworth School. There are six classrooms. How many chairs are there in total?

....

5 A car manufacturer turns out 300 cars every week at one of its factories. How many cars will be made over a period of ten years? (Take one year to be 52 weeks.)

....

6 A mountaineer needs 30 m of rope. The rope costs £3.50 per metre. Find the total cost.

....

7 Leadale School hires ten minibuses for the Year 7 outing. Each minibus takes 16 passengers plus a driver. How many people could go on the outing, including the drivers?

....

8 Rashid has £4. How many 30 p bars of chocolate can he buy?

....

9 A florist uses 80 cm of ribbon for each bouquet. At the end of one month 72 m of ribbon have been used. How many bouquets were sold that month?

....

10 An airline catering firm made 36 000 meals in a week. Each flight needs 300 meals. How many flights were made that week?

....

Links with the Classbook
Unit 1 *pages 5–6*

1.2 Addition and subtraction of whole numbers

Solve the following problems with addition or subtraction, using 'carry' or 'exchange' where necessary. A calculator should not be used.

1 Alice has three parcels to post. They weigh 342 g, 535 g and 744 g respectively. Find the total weight of the three parcels. Give your answer in grams.

....

2 The hall at Greenview School has 335 chairs. On the evening of the annual concert 432 people turn up. How many of them do not get a seat?

....

3 George is allowed to take 32 days holiday a year from his job. He goes to Malta for 11 days and to Switzerland for seven days. Does he have enough holiday left for a 15-day safari in Zimbabwe?

....

4 The numbers of pupils in three classes in Year 8 at Leadale School are 29, 31 and 32. At the beginning of term there are only 52 mathematics books in stock. How many more books must the school buy so that all the pupils in Year 8 can have their own book?

....

5 Mr and Mrs Vincent take their two children to High View Theme Park. They buy a family ticket. How much do they save by not buying separate tickets?

HIGH VIEW ADMISSION CHARGES:

Children	£4	Adults	£6
Family ticket (2 adults and up to four children)			£18

....

6 Mr Powell taught at Upworth School for 36 years. He started teaching in 1957. In what year did he leave?

....

7 Frank is on a sponsored cycle ride. When he started his mileometer read 11 326 miles, and it now reads 11 417 miles. How far has he cycled so far?

....

8 A shipping company uses containers which can take weights of up to 3050 kg. If they have already loaded 1175 kg of video equipment into a container, how much more can be loaded?

....

Links with the Classbook
Unit 1 *pages 3–5*

1.3 Professor Puzzle's maze

Professor Puzzle has hidden the key to his laboratory under one of the paving slabs of his patio.

He has drawn a map and provided clues to find out which slab it was.

Start at the top left hand corner (square A1). The answer to the question gives you a clue about where to go next.

When you have gone through all 24 squares you will end at the place where Professor Puzzle has hidden the key.

Name the square, and give the answer to the question on it.

	A	B	C	D	E	F
1	7×20	$42 + 18$	100×10	$200 \div 5$	$1240 - 99$	$210 \div 5$
2	$30 \times 31 - 30$	8×25	$3600 \div 100$	$\sqrt{900} + 5$	50×24	$\sqrt{64}$
3	$6 + 94$	$\sqrt{2500}$	$10 \div 10 - 1$	$140 - 76$	$120 \div 4$	60^2
4	$1200 \div 10$	$\sqrt[3]{1000}$	40×31	$\sqrt{36}$	35×6	$1141 + 1359$

The key is in square: ....

The answer to the question is: ....

Links with the Classbook

Unit 1
pages 3–7

1.4 Playing with numbers

Numbers such as 2 and 7 are one-digit numbers.

Numbers such as 94 and 55 are two-digit numbers.

Use this information to help you work out the answers to these questions.

1 What is the largest two-digit number?

....

2 What is the smallest four-digit number?

....

3 Write down a two-digit number which is even and also a multiple of 35.

....

4 Write down the largest four-digit number in which no digit is repeated.

....

5 What is the smallest three-digit odd number which uses the digit 1 once only?

....

6 List all the prime numbers with only one digit.

....

7 Write down the largest number you can make using all the digits from 0 to 9 without using any figure more than once.

....

Sam has these three cards:

Rana has these four cards:

Sam: 3 6 4

Rana: 0 3 2 7

8 Write down the largest three-digit number that Sam can make.

....

9 Write down the largest three-digit number that Rana can make.

....

10 What is the largest odd number that Rana can make?

....

11 Can Sam make any square numbers? If so, which?

....

12 Can Rana make any cube numbers? If so, which?

....

Links with the Classbook

Unit 1 *pages 2–3*

1.5 Left and right

Numbers in the left-hand square are multiplied by 10 to give the matching number in the right-hand square.

Fill in the missing numbers – the first one has been completed for you.

1

3	5	4	Total 12
7	2	9	18
1	6	8	15

⇨ ×10

30	50	40	Total 120
70	20	90	180
10	60	80	150

2

3		5	
	7		
4		6	

⇨ ×10

	20		
80		90	
	10		

3

2	7		10
	3	4	13
8	5		22

⇨ ×10

4

			17
			12
			16

⇨ ×10

80	40		
70		30	
	10	90	

Invent some more puzzles like these where the numbers are multiplied by 100.

Challenge your friends to solve them.

Continued on page 7.

Links with the Classbook

Unit 1
pages 5–6

1.5 Left and right continued

These puzzles are similar but this time the numbers in the left-hand square have been multiplied by 4 or by 5 to make the numbers on the right.

Fill in the missing numbers – again, the first one has been completed for you.

5

			Total
9	5	1	15
7	2	3	12
4	6	8	18

×4 ⇒

			Total
36	20	4	60
28	8	12	48
16	24	32	72

6

4		2	
	5		
	3	7	

×4 ⇒

	36		
4		32	
24			

7

4		5	10
2			13
7		6	22

×5 ⇒

	40		

8

			21
			12
			12

×4 ⇒

16	32		
24	4		
	8	12	

Invent some more puzzles like these where the numbers are multiplied by 4 or 5, or use other numbers of your choice.

Challenge your friends to solve them.

Links with the Classbook

Unit 1
pages 8–9

1.6 Number cross

Puzzle 1
Fit these numbers into the grid to make a 'number crossword'.

Here are the numbers to use:

21	131	3012	73 214
41	200	2310	
92			
97			

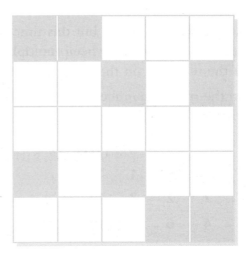

Puzzle 2
Again, fit these numbers into the grid to make a 'number crossword'. This one is a little harder.

Here are the numbers to use:

29	207	3170	10 682
60	270	5016	79 231
64	332	8219	9 701 328
72	728	8372	
91	823		
97			

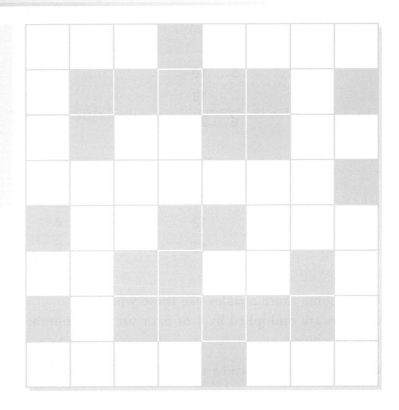

Links with the Classbook

Unit 1
pages 2–3

1.7 What is 36?

$$30 + 6 = 36$$

$$42 - 6 = 36$$

144 shared by 4 is 36

$$6 \times 6 = 36$$

$$6^2 = 36$$

$$12 \times 3 = 36$$

72 shared between 2 is 36

$$3.6 \times 10 = 36$$

36 is the number of weeks in a year take away 16

$$1 + 1 + 1 + 1 + 1 \ldots +1 = 36$$

1 See if you can make 36 by adding two numbers together.

....

2 See if you can make 36 by multiplying two numbers together.

....

3 Try to make 36 by multiplying more than 2 numbers together.

....

4 Try to make 36 by adding together some **consecutive** numbers.

....

5 Find as many ways as you can of making 36. You might like to display your ideas on a poster.

Links with the Classbook
Unit 1 *pages 8–9*

1.8 Ariadne T Adder

1	2	3	4	5	6	7	8	9	10
11	12	13	14	15	16	17	18	19	20
21	22	23	24	25	26	27	28	29	30
31	32	33	34	35	36	37	38	39	40
41	42	43	44	45	46	47	48	49	50
51	52	53	54	55	56	57	58	59	60
61	62	63	64	65	66	67	68	69	70
71	72	73	74	75	76	77	78	79	80
81	82	83	84	85	86	87	88	89	90
91	92	93	94	95	96	97	98	99	100

Ariadne is a very sleepy adder. She likes to snooze on her favourite cushion, which looks just like the number square on the left.

Sometimes she likes to lie out straight, and other times she likes to curl up, or even sleep in a zigzag shape. Ariadne lies along squares which join edge to edge, not just corner to corner.

Ariadne always takes up seven squares.

1 Draw your own number square and put in Ariadne.

2 Work out the **sum** of all the numbers Ariadne is lying on.

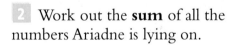

3 Keep her in the same shape, but move her **across** one square. What is the sum now?

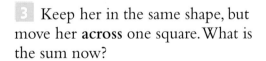

4 Work out a rule to predict what happens to the sum when Ariadne is moved across one square. Test your rule using some other starting positions.

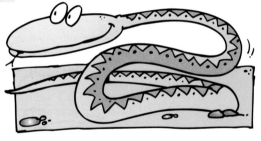

5 Now try to discover a similar rule when Ariadne moves **down** one square.

6 Look carefully at your answers to questions 4 and 5. Combine these answers to find a single rule for moving Ariadne diagonally.

Links with the Classbook
Unit 1 *pages 3–5*

Numbers and number patterns ## 2

2.1 Factors and multiples

1 Ahmed says 'I have written down a two-digit number. The number is between 40 and 50 and is a multiple of 12.' What number did Ahmed write down?

....

2 Jemma says 'I have written down a three-digit number. The number is between 110 and 120 and is a multiple of 13.' What number did Jemma write down?

....

3 Ben says 'I have written down a two-digit number which is a multiple of 9 and a factor of 36.' What number do you think Ben has written down?

....

4 What is the Lowest Common Multiple of
a) 4 and 5   **b)** 5 and 7?

....

5 What is the Highest Common Factor of
a) 30 and 75   **b)** 12 and 40?

....

> 12 is the Lowest Common Multiple of 3 and 4 because it is the smallest number which is a multiple of both 3 and 4.
>
> 6 is the Highest Common Factor of 18 and 30 because it is the largest number which is a factor of both 18 and 30.

6 Is 739 452 a multiple of 3?

....

7 Is 820 475 a multiple of 9?

....

> Professor Puzzle has found a quick way of testing whether a number is a multiple of 3:
>
> To test whether 5627 is a multiple of 3:
> 5 + 6 + 2 + 7 = 20 which is not a multiple of 3, so 5627 is not a multiple of 3
>
> To test whether 471 is multiple of 3:
> 4 + 7 + 1 = 12 which is a multiple of 3, so 471 is a multiple of 3.
>
> Professor Puzzle has found a similar way of testing for multiples of 9.
>
> Write down what this test might be and check to see if it works on the number 189.

Links with the Classbook
Unit 2 *pages* 9–11

2.2 Sequences

Explain the rule that is being used to make each of these number patterns.

Then find the next three numbers in each.

1	2	4	6	8			
2	2	4	8	16			
3	10	100	1000	10 000			
4	15	18	21	24			
5	99	94	89	84			
6	1	4	9	16			
7	5	25	125	625			
8	15	26	37	48			
9	160	80	40	20			
10	11	17	15	21	19		

Now make up five sequences of your own.

Try to catch your friends out.

11					
12					
13					
14					
15					

Links with the Classbook

Unit 2
pages 11–12

2.3 Primes and patterns

1 Find all the prime numbers between 30 and 50.

....

2 Is 83 prime or composite?

....

3 Explain how you can tell quickly that the number 243 is not prime.
[*Hint:* Remember Professor Puzzle's quick tests from the previous section.]

....

4 List all of the factors of 36. Draw a ring around those which are prime.

....

12 can be written as a product of prime numbers in the following way:

12 = 2 × 6

    = 2 × 2 × 3 or 2^2 × 3 for short.

5 Write 20 as a product of primes.

....

6 Write 26 as a product of primes.

....

Work out the rule for each of these number patterns.
Then find the next two numbers in each.

7	22	27	25	30	28	....
8	103	96	89	82	75	....
9	8	11	15	20	26	....
10	729	243	81	27	9	....

Links with the Classbook

Unit 2
pages 10–12

2.4 Baked bean tins

There are various ways that you can stack tins for display in a shop.

One of them is shown here.

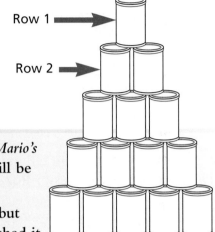

Row 1 ➡

Row 2 ➡

Marissa is creating a display for the window of *Mario's Market* and she needs to know how many tins will be used if the display is 10 rows high.

She was trying to find a pattern from this table, but went off to serve a customer before she had finished it.

1 Complete Marissa's table:

Row	Number of tins in that row	Total number of tins so far
1	1	1
2	2	3
3	3	6
4	4	
5		

Look at the pattern of numbers in the *Total number of tins so far* column.

2 How many rows would there be in a 105 tin display?

....

Continued on page 15.

Links with the Classbook

Unit 2
pages 11–12

2.4 Baked bean tins continued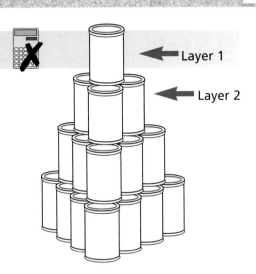

Marissa found that her stack was not very stable.

This one is more stable, but it uses more tins.

← Layer 1

← Layer 2

3 Complete this table for 10 layers:

Layer	Number of tins in that layer	Total number of tins so far
1	1	1
2	3	4
3	6	10
4	10	
5		

4 Decide which of the two displays you would use if you were the manager of *Mario's Market*. Give a reason for your answer.

....

....

....

Links with the Classbook

Unit 2
pages 11–12

2.5 Fold-ups

You will need a long strip of paper.

Fold the paper in half, then unfold it again. Count the number of creases.

1 crease

Fold the paper again, in the same direction. Count the number of creases.

3 creases

Work out how many creases there will be if you could fold the paper 10 times.

[*Hint:* After the first 3 or 4 folds you will find it very difficult to fold the paper any more, so you will have to solve this problem by looking at the number patterns which you have obtained so far.]

Links with the Classbook

Unit 2
pages 11–12

2.6 Circle sections

If you draw a circle and split it by drawing one line through it ...

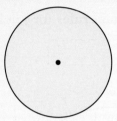   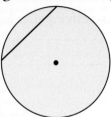

... you can see that it is divided into two regions.

If you draw another line across the circle ...

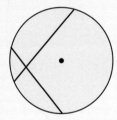

... you can divide it into four regions.

Draw some more diagrams, and record your results in this table:

Number of lines	Number of regions
0	1
1	2
2	4
3	

[*Hint:* After the first few lines be very careful – the idea is to get the **maximum** number of sections as you add each new line. Make sure that you do not 'lose' any regions by having three lines crossing over at the same point. Don't try to draw too many diagrams – you can use the number patterns to help you.]

How many sections will there be if you draw 10 lines?

....

Links with the Classbook
Unit 2 *pages* 11–12

2.7 Epicycloids

Epicycloids are circle patterns.

You can create some attractive patterns by following certain rules for joining up the points.

1 Join 1 to 2,
   2 to 4,
   3 to 6 and so on.

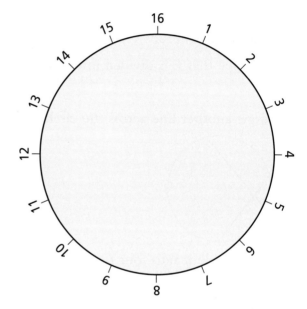

2 Join 1 to 3,
   2 to 6,
   3 to 9 and so on.

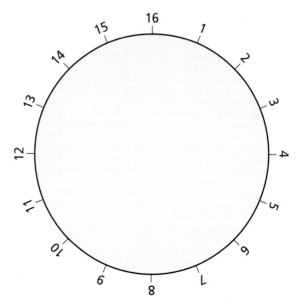

Continued on page 18.

2.7 Epicycloids continued

Does it make any difference if you use a circle with 36 points instead of 16?
Try it and see.

3 Join 1 to 2,
      2 to 4,
      3 to 6 and so on.

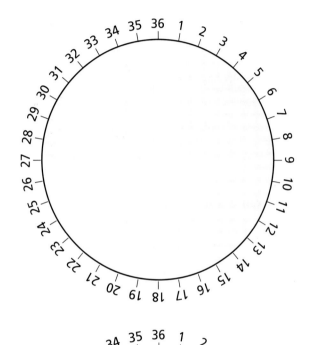

4 Join 1 to 3,
      2 to 6,
      3 to 9 and so on.

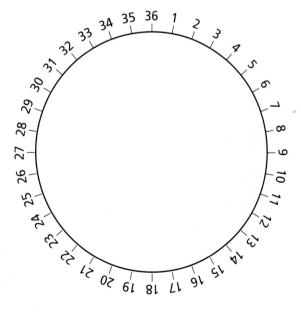

Now experiment with some
ideas of your own.

Links with the Classbook
Unit 2 *pages 8–9*

2.8 Ariadne multiples

1	2	3	4	5	6	7	8	9	10
11	12	13	14	15	16	17	18	19	20
21	22	23	24	25	26	27	28	29	30
31	32	33	34	35	36	37	38	39	40
41	42	43	44	45	46	47	48	49	50
51	52	53	54	55	56	57	58	59	60
61	62	63	64	65	66	67	68	69	70
71	72	73	74	75	76	77	78	79	80
81	82	83	84	85	86	87	88	89	90
91	92	93	94	95	96	97	98	99	100

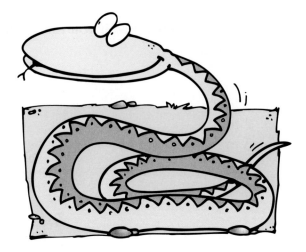

Do you remember Ariadne?

She wants to lie on this number square in which all the multiples of 3 have been coloured. Sometimes she likes to lie out straight, and other times she likes to curl up, or even sleep in a zigzag shape.

Ariadne always takes up seven squares.

1 What is the smallest number of coloured squares she can lie on?

....

2 What is the largest number of coloured squares she can lie on?

....

3 If Ariadne has to lie on exactly three coloured squares, in how many different positions can she lie?

....

4 Explore what happens if you use multiples of 4 instead.

....
....

5 Explore what happens if you use multiples of 5 instead.

....
....

Links with the Classbook

Unit 2
pages 8–9

3.1 Problems with fractions

In all of these problems give answers which are fractions in their simplest form.

1 What fraction is coloured in each of these diagrams?

a)

b)

c)

a) .... b) .... c) ....

2 Sacheen had 15 sweets and gave one-third to her brother Paul.

a) What fraction did she have left? ....

b) How many sweets did she have left? ....

3 Freddie earned himself some extra pocket money by washing cars. If he spent $\frac{2}{5}$ on a magazine and $\frac{1}{5}$ on sweets, what fraction of the money did he have left to save?

....

4 The pupils in Year 5 at Greenview School carried out a survey on hair colour. They found that $\frac{1}{5}$ of the pupils had blonde hair, $\frac{1}{10}$ had auburn hair and the rest various shades of brown. What fraction had brown hair?
[*Hint:* Change $\frac{1}{5}$ into tenths first.]

....

5 Cressy is going to have 12 months off between school and university. She plans to spend half of it travelling, one third working, and the rest of it doing unpaid work experience.

a) How many months will she spend on each activity?

....

b) What fraction will she spend on work experience? ....

Links with the Classbook

Unit 3
pages 15–17

3.2 Percentage problems

1 Shade 75% of this shape.

2 Shade 40% of this shape.

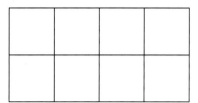

3 What percentage of this shape has been shaded?

....

4 What percentage is 32 out of 100?

....

5 Aurelius achieved 29 out of 50 in a French verb test. What percentage is this?

....

6 Zia thinks that 45% is the same as $\frac{9}{20}$. Is she right?

....

7 Jon scores 17 out of 40 in a mathematics test. He tells his friends that his score is 35%. Is he right?

....

8 Lorien has £1000 in a building society account. After one year she receives 5% of this amount as interest. How much interest does Lorien receive?

....

9 Boxes of 'Chunky Chocolates' contain 20% soft-centred sweets and 30% toffee-centred sweets. There are 30 sweets in each box.
a) How many sweets have soft centres?
b) How many sweets have toffee centres?

....

....

10 Anya achieved 72% in her German exam. The exam was marked out of 50. How many marks did Anya score in the exam?

....

Links with the Classbook

Unit 3
pages 17–18

3.3 Calcucross

Change these fractions into percentages. Then write the percentages in the grid.

Across		Down	
2 $\frac{32}{100}$	**8** $\frac{28}{50}$	**1** $\frac{11}{100}$	**6** $\frac{18}{50}$
4 $\frac{3}{2}$	**9** $\frac{250}{200}$	**2** $\frac{33}{11}$	**7** $\frac{330}{300}$
5 $\frac{9}{12}$	**11** $\frac{4}{5}$	**3** $\frac{3}{20}$	**8** $\frac{11}{20}$
		5 $\frac{45}{60}$	**10** $\frac{14}{25}$

Links with the Classbook

Unit 3
pages 17–18

3.4 Misprints

Spokes Card Game Company have produced a new card game. Players have to collect sets of five cards with equivalent fractions on them.

Here is one set of five cards:

$$\frac{1}{4} \qquad \frac{2}{8} \qquad \frac{3}{12} \qquad \frac{4}{16} \qquad \frac{8}{32}$$

Unfortunately no one checked the cards for accuracy before they were printed, and two of the cards are printed incorrectly.

The full set of cards, mixed up, are shown below. Draw circles round the two incorrect cards.

Links with the Classbook

Unit 3 pages 16–17

Working with decimals

4.1 Changing units

1. Write 734 mm in centimetres.

   ....

2. Write 503 cm in metres.

   ....

3. Henrietta measured the length and breadth of her desk as 1230 mm and 623 mm. Write these measurements in centimetres.

   ....

4. Ken is designing some shelves. He wants them to be 78.5 cm long and 25.5 cm wide. Write these measurements in millimetres.

   ....

5. Sadie can throw the javelin 10.76 m. How far is this in centimetres?

   ....

6. Colleen is making some curtains, which are 132 cm long. Write this measurement in metres.

   ....

7. Georgie is 1.34 m tall. Change her height into centimetres.

   ....

8. Afam jumps 432 cm in the long jump on sports day. Write this length in metres.

   ....

9. Kira measures the length of her thumb as 61 mm. Write this in centimetres.

   ....

10. Alex can jump 1.87 m in the high jump. Write this height in centimetres.

   ....

Links with the Classbook
Unit 4 *pages 22–23*

4.2 Money problems

1 Lucy has £4.50 pocket money, and her uncle sends her £5 as a present. How much money does Lucy now have?

....

2 Samir bought a magazine for £1.99 and a bar of chocolate for 28p. How much money did he spend altogether?

....

3 Bryony is sending two parcels to her cousins in Australia. One will cost £3.25 to post, while the other will cost £2.80. How much does she spend on postage in total?

....

4 David owes £5.75 to Ben and £6.50 to William. His grandfather has just sent him £20. How much will David have left once he has repaid his debts?

....

5 Charlie buys a new tennis racket at £45.99 and trainers for £27.50. She also buys a box of four tennis balls for £9.99. How much does she spend altogether?

....

Links with the Classbook
Unit 4 *pages 22–23*

6 Dan has earned £35 and is going to treat himself to an evening out. If his train fare is £7.80 and the concert ticket costs £12, how much money does he have left to buy himself a meal?

....

7 Pip has been shopping. She had £45 to start with and came back with £13.94. How much did she spend?

....

8 Vish is paying the month's bills. He has a phone bill of £28.56, a gas bill of £18.72 and an electricity bill of £21.35. What is the total amount of his three bills?

....

9 Stacey, Clare and Louise have won a lottery prize worth £126.60. If they share it equally how much will each of them have won?

....

10 Claire, Kate and Matt have been busy earning extra pocket money doing odd jobs. They earned £12.60, £15 and £10.50 respectively. If they pool the money and then share it out equally how much will each get?

....

4.3 Weights and measures

1 Felicity has a piece of string 1.95 m long. She cuts off lengths of 35 cm, 65 cm and 23 cm. How much string will be left over?

....

2 Aaron and Sam are going on a hike. They plan to walk 7.5 km on the first day, 10.3 km on the second and 9.4 km on the third. How far are they going to walk altogether?

....

3 Richard bakes a cake, using 0.25 kg of flour, 0.2 kg of margarine, 0.2 kg of sugar and four eggs which weigh 0.3 kg altogether. Find the total weight of all the ingredients.

....

4 Three suitcases weigh 20 kg in total; two of them are 11.4 kg and 4.7 kg. Find the weight of the third suitcase.

....

5 In a triathlon Andrew ran 15.5 km, swam 2.4 km and cycled 24.7 km. What distance did he cover in total?

....

6 Emma has 3.5 m of material and needs 1.6 m for a skirt and 1.15 m for a jacket.
a) Find the total length of material Emma needs. ....

b) Does she have enough material left over to make a waistcoat needing 0.9 m of material?

....

7 Baby Tom weighed 2.3 kg when he was born. When he was six months old he weighed 5.9 kg. How much weight did he gain during this time?

....

8 At Easter Sara bought each of her cousins a bag of sweets. They weighed 0.25 kg, 0.5 kg, 0.35 kg and 0.42 kg. What was the total weight of all four bags?

....

9 Marcel wants to cut some lengths of drainpipe. He has 7.2 m of suitable pipe. He needs to cut three pieces, of lengths 1.4 m, 0.9 m and 1.65 m. How much pipe will he have left over?

....

10 Mark's granny knits him a jumper. She uses 0.25 kg of red wool, 0.05 kg of white wool and 0.3 kg of blue wool. What is the weight of the finished jumper?

....

Links with the Classbook
Unit 4 *pages 22–23*

4.4 Place values in decimals

1 In a length of 1.92 m, the 9 represents 9 tenths of a metre while the 2 represents 2 hundredths of a metre. For each of the measurements below write down the part of a metre represented by the underlined digit:
a) 1.4<u>8</u> m **b)** 18.<u>6</u>9 m **c)** 0.2<u>7</u> m

a) ....
b) ....
c) ....

2 For each of these measurements write down the part of a centimetre represented by the underlined digit:
a) 10.<u>1</u> cm **b)** 19.5<u>6</u> cm **c)** 6.0<u>8</u> cm

a) ....
b) ....
c) ....

3 Write all these measurements in centimetres. Then write them down in order of size, starting with the largest one.
12.4 m 1.2 m 3.07 m 3.72 m 2.14 m

....
....

4 Write down these measurements in order of size, starting with the smallest.
2.4 m 2.04 m 20.4 cm
20.44 m 2.04 cm

....
....

5 Write these weights in order of size, giving the largest first.
1.3 kg 1.03 kg 2.6 kg
1.33 kg 2.61 kg

....
....

6 Which is the odd one out?
3.4 m 340 cm 3.40 m
3400 mm 3.04 m

....
....

7 Which is the odd one out?
702 cm 7.2 m 7200 mm
7.20 m 720 cm

....
....

8 Which is the longest measurement?
6.09 m 699 cm 6.9 m
609 cm 6.99 cm

....
....

Links with the Classbook
Unit 4 *pages* 21–23

4.5 Decimal cover-up

This is a game for two players.

The idea is to cover up a complete line of squares – vertical, horizontal or diagonal.

Rules

The first player chooses one blue card and one white card, and adds up the numbers on them (without a calculator).

The second player checks the answer on a calculator.

If the answer is correct the first player can claim the square with that answer on it.

Now the second player chooses two numbers, and the game continues.

The first person to complete four in a row is the winner.

Be careful – not all combinations appear in the grid.

| 0.95 | 4.56 | 3.74 | 5.5 | 3.11 |

| 4.2 | 1.9 | 2.5 | 1.5 | 0.62 |

1.57	7.06	6.46	2.85
4.61	6.12	5.24	2.45
6.06	5.18	3.73	5.61
8.76	5.64	5.15	6.24

Links with the Classbook

Unit 4
pages 23–24

5.1 Mapping islands

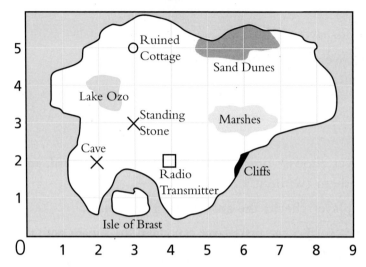

Use the map above to answer the following questions.

1 What is at the point with coordinates (2, 4)?

....

2 What is the ground like at (6, 3)?

....

3 Why might you want a torch if you were at the point with coordinates (2, 2)?

....

4 Why would you not like to walk around blindfold near the point (6, 2)?

....

5 What are the coordinates of the radio transmitter?

....

6 What is at the point with coordinates (3, 5) ?

....

7 If you started at (4, 3) and travelled to (3, 1) why might you need a boat?

....

8 What are the coordinates of the standing stone?

....

Links with the Classbook

Unit 5 *pages 26–29*

5.2 Coordinates and codes

Use the grid below to work out the message which has been coded in coordinates. Each word is separated by a dash.

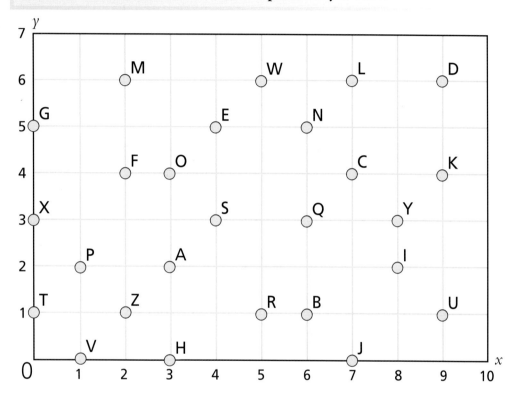

The message:

(5, 6) (3, 0) (4, 5) (6, 5) / (8, 3) (3, 4) (9, 1) / (3, 0) (3, 2) (1, 0) (4, 5) /

(2, 4) (8, 2) (6, 5) (8, 2) (4, 3) (3, 0) (4, 5) (9, 6) / (0, 1) (3, 0) (8, 2) (4, 3) /

(6, 3) (9, 1) (4, 5) (4, 3) (0, 1) (8, 2) (3, 4) (6, 5) / (2, 6) (3, 2) (9, 4) (4, 5) /

(9, 1) (1, 2) / (3, 2) / (7, 4) (3, 4) (9, 6) (4, 5) / (2, 4) (3, 4) (5, 1) /

(8, 3) (3, 4) (9, 1) (5, 1) / (2, 4) (5, 1) (8, 2) (4, 5) (6, 5) (9, 6) /

The message is: ....

....

....

....

Links with the Classbook

Unit 5
pages 26–29

5.3 Wibbly-wobbly

Draw a picture on this ordinary grid

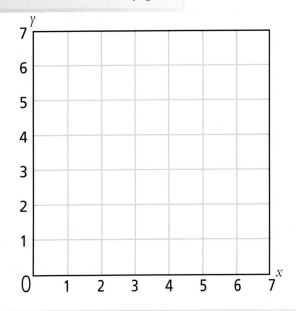

Now swap books with a friend and get them to transfer your picture onto this Wibbly-wobbly grid:

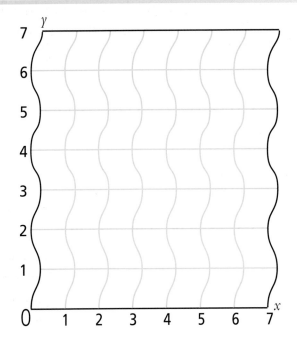

Links with the Classbook

Unit 5
pages 30–31

5.4 Missing the point

For each of these questions draw a grid so that *x* and *y* can each run from 0 to 10. Plot the given points, and work out where each missing one must be.

Draw a fresh grid for each question.

Work on squared paper.

1 ABCD is a square, A is at (1, 4), B is at (1, 6), C is at (3, 6). Where is D?

....

2 MNPQ is a rectangle, M is at (3, 6), N is at (7, 6), P is at (7, 4). Where is Q?

....

3 STUV is a kite, S is at (4, 6), T is at (5, 3), U is at (5, 7). Where is V?

....

4 WXYZ is a parallelogram, W is at (0, 0), X is at (5, 0), Z is at (2, 4). Where is Y?

....

5 FGH is a right-angled triangle, F is at (4, 4), G is at (4, 8). There are lots of different places that the point H could be. Given that the line GH is 3 units long suggest what the coordinates of H might be.

....

6 JKLM is a parallelogram, J is at (1, 3), K is at (3, 5) , L is at (7, 5). What are the coordinates of M ?

....

7 One vertex (or corner) of a square is at (2, 2), the oppposite vertex is at (6, 6). What are the co-ordinates of the other two vertices ?

....

8 The points R, S and T all lie on a straight line. R is at (2, 3), S is at (5, 5) and T is at (8, *y*). What is the value of *y*?

....

Links with the Classbook

Unit 5
pages 30–31

5.5 Bang in the middle

On the grid draw a set of axes so that x and y can each run from 0 to 10.

Plot the given pairs of points, and join each pair with a straight line.

Measure each line with a ruler and work out the coordinates of the **midpoint** (the point midway between the two ends of the line).

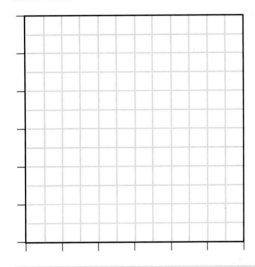

1 (0, 0) and (4, 4) ....

2 (0, 4) and (6, 4) ....

3 (0, 2) and (4, 8) ....

4 (1, 7) and (3, 3) ....

5 (5, 1) and (3, 5) ....

Look at the coordinates of the ends of each line and the coordinates of the midpoints of each line.

Can you see any connection between them?

Try and write down a rule for finding the midpoint of a line which joins two points.

Don't plot the points in questions 6–10 but use your rule to work out the coordinates of the midpoints of the lines joining them.

6 (0, 0) and (6, 6)

....

7 (2, 2) and (8, 8)

....

8 (2, 10) and (6, 2)

....

9 (3, 1) and (9, 5)

....

10 (7, 1) and (3, 7)

....

Links with the Classbook
Unit 5 *pages* 30–31

6.1 Reflection symmetry

This shape
is almost
symmetrical...

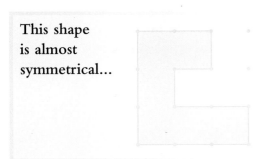

...and we
can give it
reflection
symmetry
by adding
one square.

Make these shapes symmetrical in the
same way. Add only one square to each.

Links with the
Classbook

Unit 6
pages 34–36

6.2 Rotation symmetry

Some of these shapes have rotational symmetry, others do not.

For those which do have rotational symmetry:
● mark the centre of rotation
● write down the order of rotational symmetry.

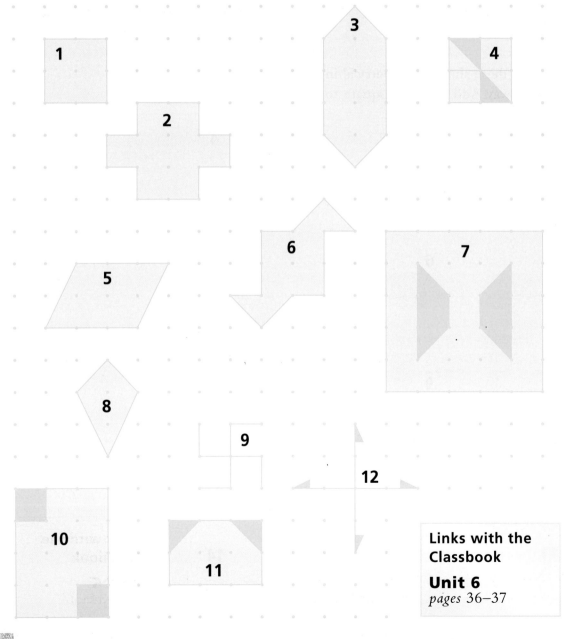

Links with the Classbook

Unit 6
pages 36–37

6.3 Congruent shapes

This shape...   ...can be divided into two **congruent** pieces.

Each of the shapes below can be divided into two congruent pieces.

Use a pencil to draw a line on each shape showing how this can be done.

There is more than one way to do some of them.

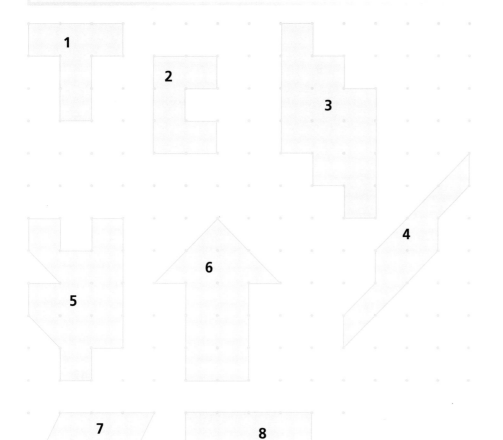

Now try to create some other shapes like these. Try them out on your friends

Links with the Classbook
Unit 6
pages 38–39

6.4 Making squares

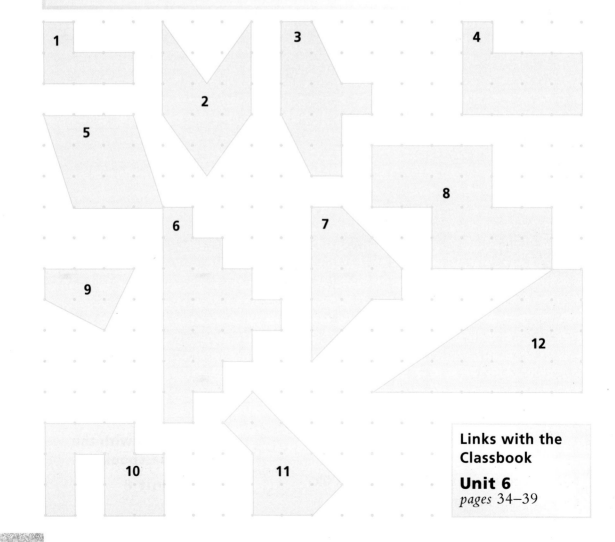

| 1. A shape | 2. One cut | 3. Rearrange | 4. Square |

Each of the shapes below can be rearranged to make a square.

You only need one cut, as in the example above.

Use a pencil to show how the shapes should be split.

Links with the Classbook

Unit 6
pages 34–39

6.5 One-word answers

1 Three-wheeled pedal powered vehicle

tricycle
....

2 Three-sided polygon

....

3 Three sisters born on the same day

....

4 Four-footed animal

....

5 Four brothers born on the same day

....

6 Multiply by four

....

7 Four-sided polygon

....

8 Athletic contest with five events

....

9 Five-sided polygon

....

10 Group of six musicians

....

11 Six-sided polygon

....

12 Eight-legged sea creature

....

13 Eighth month of the Roman year

....

14 Eight-faced polyhedron

....

15 Ten years

....

16 Athletic contest with ten events

....

17 One hundred years

....

18 Commander of one hundred men in the Roman army

....

19 A thousand years

....

Links with the Classbook
Unit 6 *pages 39–41*

6.6 Tessellations

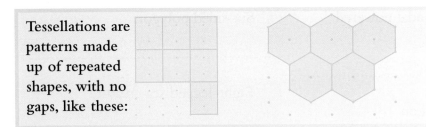

Tessellations are patterns made up of repeated shapes, with no gaps, like these:

Make copies of each of these shapes on isometric paper.
Show how each one tessellates by adding more shapes to your diagram. You should use at least 10 of each shape.

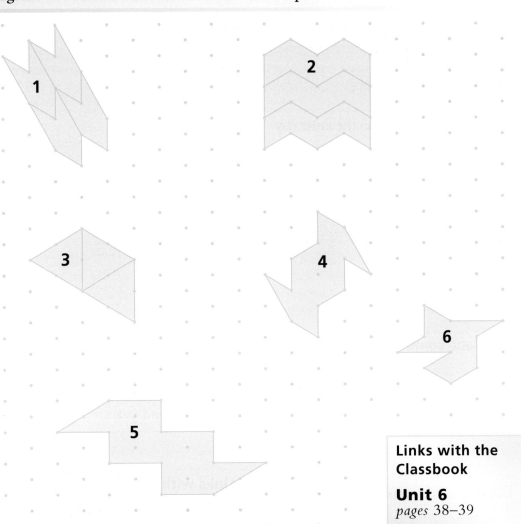

Links with the Classbook

Unit 6
pages 38–39

6.7 Trisides

1 On isometric paper draw a triangle and mark the mid point of each side.

2 Add a shape to half of one side.

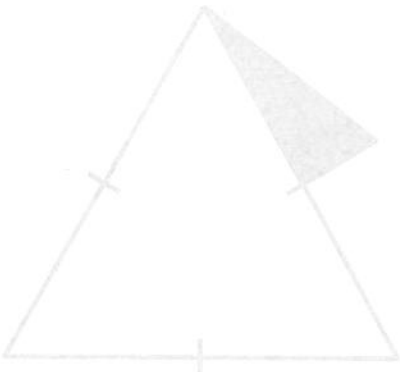

3 Rotate the added piece through 180° around the midpoint of the side. Mark the new position. The piece added to one half of the side is taken off the other half.

4 Repeat using other shapes on the other two sides.

This new shape is called a TRISIDE and will tessellate.

Is the area of the new shape the same as the area of the original one?

Make a template of your triside and design a tessellating pattern.

Here's one idea.

Links with the Classbook

Unit 6
pages 38–39

6.8. Euler's Relation

Leonhard Euler (pronounced 'oiler') was born in Switzerland in 1707. He is famous for his mathematics, in particular the way he used symbols.

He discovered a simple relation between the number of vertices, edges and faces of 3-D shapes. See if you can work out what it is.

Complete the table.

Shape		Vertices (V)	Edges (E)	Faces (F)	$V - E + F$
Cube		8			
Tetrahedron			6		
Octahedron				8	
Icosahedron		12	30	20	12 – 30 + 20 =2
Dodecahedron					

1 What do you notice about the expression $V - E + F$? What is Euler's Relation?

....

....

2 Investigate for other 3-D shapes, for example cuboids, prisms and so on. Does Euler's Relation apply to these shapes too?

....

Links with the Classbook

Unit 6
pages 39–41

7.1 What's best?

For each of these quantities decide which is the better measurement to use.

1. The length of a car (metres or centimetres).

....

2. The weight of a bag of potatoes (kilograms or grams).

....

3. The distance from London to Gatwick (kilometres or metres).

....

4. The time taken to run 200 m (seconds or minutes).

....

5. The amount of liquid in a glass (millilitres or litres).

....

Estimate the following measurements in metric units:

6. The height of a lamp post.

....

7. The weight of a large bunch of bananas.

....

8. The height of a door.

....

9. The time taken to count to 150.

....

10. The volume of liquid in a full coffee mug.

....

Here are two problems to solve about liquid and capacity.

11. There are five buckets in a row, the first three are full of water and the other two are empty. By moving only one bucket is it possible to make the buckets go alternately full, empty, full, empty, full?

....

12. If you have a five-litre jug, a two-litre jug and as much water as you like, is it possible to measure out exactly one litre of water ?

....

Links with the Classbook

Unit 7
page 45

7.2 Reading scales

Read the values on these scales.

Write your answers to a sensible level of accuracy.

1

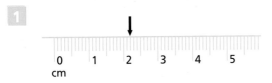

....

2

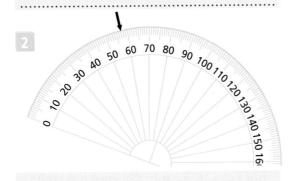

....

3

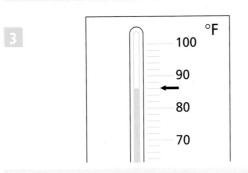

....

4

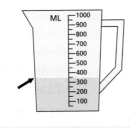

....

5

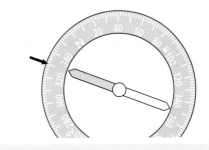

....

6

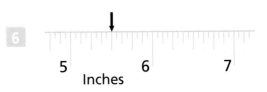

....

7

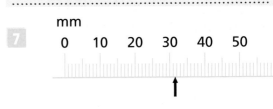

....

8

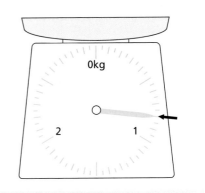

....

Links with the Classbook

Unit 7
pages 46

7.3 Inappropriate measures

Look at the following sentences and change the length, weight or capacity into a more appropriate unit.

1 Zoë measured a piece of string and found that it was 1230 mm long.

....

2 Joe bought a bag of potatoes that weighed 1500 g.

....

3 Rana has been on a run and she has estimated that she went 3200 m.

....

4 Jake has measured the length of his stride and found that it is 0.000 63 km.

....

5 Martin shares a bag of sweets with his sister. He has weighed them and they each have 0.035 kg.

....

6 Susie has been swimming at the local pool where each length is 2500 cm.

....

7 Zac weighs 35 730 g.

....

8 Chris is trying to estimate the height of a tree in his back garden. He says that it is 0.0195 km high.

....

9 Mars bars should weigh about 0.065 kg.

....

10 Rachael's baby brother weighed 0.0032 tonnes when he was born.

....

11 Abdul has a bottle of coke. It contains 2000 ml.

....

12 Esther lives 348 200 cm away from her best friend.

....

> **Links with the Classbook**
>
> **Unit 7**
> pages 44–45

7.4 There's a time for everything ...

Look at the following sentences and change the times into more appropriate units.

1 Sarah phoned her mother and said that she would be home in 900 seconds.

....

2 Linda has to take a biology exam which will be 135 minutes long.

....

3 Samantha and her brother Jonathon are going on holiday for 240 hours.

....

4 Lee is going to visit a friend for a week. It will take him 0.25 of a day to get there.

....

5 Rana says that it will take her 1800 seconds to walk home from work.

....

6 Paul and Rashid are having a competition to see who can put up a tent faster. It takes Paul 0.1 of an hour and it takes Rashid 350 seconds. Who was faster ?

....

7 Sean is writing an essay. He reckons that it will take him 210 minutes.

....

8 It takes 3600 seconds for a train to get from Horsham to London Victoria.

....

9 Guy and Sarah have cooked a meal. It has taken them 1320 seconds.

....

10 Richard is 288 months old.

....

11 Marion is watching a TV programme which is 2400 seconds long.

....

12 Dave has lived in the same house for 182 weeks.

....

Links with the Classbook

Unit 7
pages 44–45

7.5 The school bus

The bus which goes past Greenview School stops at various places on the way.

The first bus leaves Castle Street at 7.40 a.m. and they leave at 20-minute intervals after that.

Castle Street	7.40	8.00			9.00		9.40
Park Place	7.48						
Larnett Square		8.15					
West Road		8.24					
Telford Lane	8.09						

1 Fill in the gaps in the timetable above.

2 Greenview school is a 15-minute walk from the West Road stop and a five-minute walk from the Telford Lane stop. Which would be the best place to get off if you were late for school ?

....

In the afternoons the buses leave Telford Lane at 3.15 p.m. and every 20 minutes after that.

Each section of the journey takes the same length of time as in the morning.

Telford Lane	3.15	3.35			
West Road					
Larnett Square					
Park Place					
Castle Street					

3 Fill in the gaps in the second timetable.

4 Sanjay arrives at the Larnett Square bus stop at 4.00 p.m. and catches the next bus to come along. If the bus is on time, what time will he arrive at Castle Street?

Links with the Classbook

Unit 7
pages 44–45

....

7.6 TV times

BBC 1	BBC 2	ITV	Channel 4
5.10pm Blue Peter	3.30pm International	5.10pm Home and Away	4.00pm Fifteen to one
5.35pm Neighbours	tennis	5.35pm Early evening news	4.40pm Countdown
6.00pm 6 o'clock news	6.00pm Gardener's World	6.00pm Regional news	4.55pm Ricki Lake
6.30pm Regional news	6.30pm Star Trek	7.00pm Emmerdale	6.00pm Roseanne
7.00pm Auntie's Bloomers	7.20pm The Simpsons	7.30pm Coronation Street	7.00pm Hollyoaks
7.30pm Tomorrow's World	8.00pm University	8.00pm Inspector Morse	7.30pm Channel 4 news
8.00pm Children's Hospital	Challenge	10.00pm The 10 o'clock	8.05pm Real Gardens
8.30pm As time goes by	8.30pm Changing Rooms	news	9.00pm Howard's End
9.00pm 9 o'clock news	9.00pm Top Gear		(film)
9.30pm Match of the Day	10.00pm The Chart Show		11.00pm Late evening news
10.30pm Film '98	10.30pm Newsnight		

Use this extract from a TV guide to answer the following questions.

1 What is on BBC2 at 8.00 p.m. ?

....

2 When would a cartoon fan want to watch television?

....

3 Is it possible to watch the whole of 'Coronation Street' and 'The Simpsons'?

....

4 Which channel would a film buff want to watch at 9.00 p.m.?

....

5 There are two programmes which would be popular with gardeners. What time are they, and on which channels ?

....

....

6 Damian wants to record 'The Simpsons' and 'The Chart Show'. He has an hour and a half left on a video tape. Is the tape long enough ? Explain your answer.

....

7 What is the total amount of time given to sport on BBC 1 and BBC2 ?

....

8 Debbie switches on Channel 4 at a quarter past five. What programme is on, and how long is it altogether?

....

9 Richard's train gets in at 8.06 p.m. and it takes him 20 minutes to walk home. Will he be home in time for 'As time goes by' ?

....

8.1 Perimeter

Find the perimeter of each of these shapes.

1

....

2

....

3

....

4

....

Complete these shapes so that they have the stated perimeter.

5

Perimeter 12

6

Perimeter 20

7

Perimeter 14

8

Perimeter 18

9

Perimeter 16

10

Perimeter 24

Links with the Classbook

Unit 8 *pages* 48–50

8.2 Area

Work out the areas of each of these shapes by counting up
the whole squares and half squares.

1

Area: ....

2

Area: ....

3

Area: ....

4

Area: ....

Complete these shapes so that they have the stated area.

5

area 10

6

area 14

7

area 12

8

area 16

9

area 8

10

area 7

Links with the Classbook
Unit 8 *page* 51

8.3 Isometric drawings

Here is an isometric drawing of a
1 × 1 × 1 cube.

1 On isometric paper draw a 2 × 2 × 2 cube.

Here is an isometric drawing of a
1 × 1 × 5 cuboid. It contains
five small cubes.

2 Copy this drawing onto isometric
paper and complete it so that it looks like
an upside-down letter 'L'. Your drawing
should contain seven small cubes.

3 Redraw the shape you have just drawn but this time add to it,
to make a letter 'F'.

4 Now make an isometric drawing of a letter 'E'.

Make isometric drawings of as many other letters as you
can. Be warned – they are not all as easy as you might
think. If you get stuck, try 'H' or 'U' to begin with.

**Links with the
Classbook**

Unit 8
pages 53–54

8.4 Volume

In these isometric drawings one small cube represents one cubic centimetre.
For each object find the volume and also the total area of the outside surfaces.

1

volume: ....

area: ....

2

volume: ....   area: ....

3

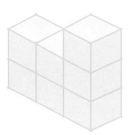

volume: ....   area: ....

4

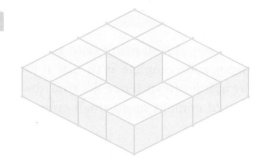

volume: ....   area: ....

5

volume: ....   area: ....

6

volume: ....

area: ....

Links with the Classbook

Unit 8
pages 51–54

8.5 Gnome homes

Gnomes live in houses made out of *four* small cubes.

The diagram shows one possible design for a Gnome Home.

You could make models of Gnome Homes using *'Digifix'* cubes.

1 On isometric paper design and draw as many Gnome Homes as you can think of . . . there are lots!

2 If it costs a gnome ⅋3 to paint each face of a 'digifix' cube on the outside of his Gnome Home, find and draw the cheapest shape of home to paint. (⅋3 means 3 gnomers – the gnomes' unit of currency.)

In addition to this, a gnome also has to pay a ground rent of ⅋6 for each square face which touches the ground.

3 Which shape of home is the cheapest now ?

4 Draw the home which is now the most expensive.

If two gnomes share a home, they are able to live in one made out of six 'digifix' cubes.

5 Assuming that paint costs the same and the ground rent is the same, how much cheaper could it be for two gnomes to share a home rather than living separately ?

....

Links with the Classbook

Unit 8
pages 51–54

8.6 Painted squares

If you look at this square you can see that it has been split into lots of smaller squares.

Some of these smaller squares have two sides on the outside of the big square, some have one side on the outside and some do not have any on the outside.

The outside of the big square has been painted, as shown by the blue line.

1   How many small squares have no sides painted?   ....

2   How many small squares have one side painted?   ....

3   How many small squares have two sides painted?   ....

4   Fill in the table for squares with up to six squares on each side.

Number of squares along each side	No sides painted	1 side painted	2 sides painted	Total number of squares
2				
3				
4				16
5				
6				

5   Why do you think the 1 × 1 square has not been included in this table ?

....

Links with the Classbook
Unit 8 *pages* 48–50

6   Look at the number patterns in each column. See if you can work out the next few numbers in each column. Can you predict the numbers for a square which has 10 squares on each side ?

....

7   Explore what happens if you use a large rectangle instead of a large square.

9.1 Mode and median

1 The number of goals scored in seven football matches were 3, 5, 7, 2, 2, 2 and 4. Find the mode and the median.

mode: .... median: ....

2 Five friends were discussing the number of brothers and sisters they each had. The numbers were 1, 0, 4, 2, 1. Find the mode and the median of these numbers.

mode: .... median: ....

3 Annie was telling Jemma about the number of chocolate bars she had eaten over the past week. The numbers for the seven days were 3, 2, 4, 0, 2, 1 and 2. Find the mode and median of these numbers.

mode: .... median: ....

4 The U13 rounders team were reviewing the number of rounders they had scored over the season. The scores for the past nine matches were 2, 4, 5, 3, 6, 8, 3, 4 and 3. Calculate the median and mode of their scores.

mode: .... median: ....

5 Philip and Tamsin were comparing their exam results. Their percentages were as follows:

	Mathematics	French	English	History	Science
Philip	88	35	93	81	48
Tamsin	90	68	75	85	80

a) Find the median score for each pupil.

Philip: .... Tamsin: ....

b) Do you think the medians provide a sensible way of comparing their ability? Explain your answer.

....

....

Links with the Classbook

Unit 9
pages 58–59

9.2 Tallies and tables

1 The pupils in Mr Taylor's class did a mental arithmetic test. The test was out of 20 and their scores were:

16 12 18 20 12 15 16 15 13 17 19 20 15 13
12 15 13 15 14 14 18 19 20 18 16 12 17 20

a) Fill in the frequency table for these 28 scores.
b) State the value of the mode.

Score	Tally	Frequency
12		
13		
14		
15		
16		
17		
18		
19		
20		

2 Dan did a survey about the colours of the cars which drove past his house between 5 p.m. and 5.15 p.m. one evening. He summarised his results in the frequency table below:

Between 5.15 p.m. and 5.20 p.m. he saw two more red cars, four green cars, one black car and three blue cars.

a) Draw up a new frequency table to show the results for the whole twenty minutes that he was watching.

b) State the mode of the complete set of data.

c) Display the data, using a vertical line graph.

Colour of car	Frequency
Blue	5
Red	2
Green	6
White	3
Black	7
Yellow	1
Silver	3

Colour of car	Frequency
Blue	
Red	
Green	
White	
Black	
Yellow	
Silver	

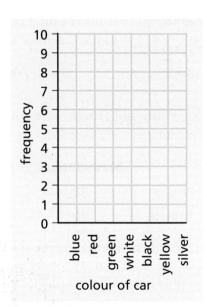

Links with the Classbook
Unit 9 *pages 59–61*

9.3 Feet and fingers

Here are two tasks which will involve your whole class.

Task 1: Feet

Ask everyone in your class what size shoes they take. Fill in the table.

1 Find the mode and the median of your data.

mode:............................ median:........................

2 Display the information using a vertical line graph.

3 What sort of person do you think might want to collect data about shoe sizes?

....

Shoe size	Tally	Frequency
1		
2		
3		
4		
5		
6		
7		
8		
9		
10		
11		

Task 2: Fingers

Measure the length of the longest right-hand finger of everyone in your class. Record the results in the table.

Length (cm)	Tally	Frequency
6.0 cm up to just under 6.5 cm		
6.5 cm up to just under 7.0 cm		

4 State the modal class for your data. ....

5 Display the information using a suitable graph.

6 Do you think it is easier to collect information about shoe sizes or finger lengths? ....

7 Explain why finger lengths cannot really be displayed in a simple vertical line graph.

....

Links with the Classbook
Unit 9 *pages 58–62*

10 Introducing probability

10.1 Is it likely?

For each of the following scenarios say whether the outcome is likely, has an even chance, is unlikely or whether you don't know without more information.

1 Jacqueline throws two dice and gets two sixes.

....

2 Paul has six blue socks and six red socks in a drawer. He picks one at random and it is red.

....

3 Year 3 at Greenview School have a mathematics lesson some time this week.

....

4 Usha has a bag with one yellow counter and twelve blue counters in it. She chooses one counter at random and it is yellow.

....

5 Rajit decides to wear a pair of green shorts.

....

6 Doreen tosses a coin and gets heads.

....

7 Phillip has 20 cards numbered 1 to 20. He picks one at random and gets a multiple of 9.

....

8 Tim shuffles a pack of cards. He picks one at random and finds that it is red.

....

9 Farnborough town football club win the FA cup final.

....

10 Joy has a purse full of coins. She takes one out at random and finds that it is a 5p piece.

....

11 Mr Todd, who buys one National Lottery ticket every week, will not win this Saturday.

....

12 Two dice are thrown and the sum of the numbers is even.

....

> **Links with the Classbook**
>
> **Unit 10**
> *pages 66–68*

10.2 Are you sure?

Look at the five situations described below, then write the
letters A, B, C, D and E in the correct rows of the table.

A When you toss a coin you get tails.

B When you throw a dice you will get a 6.

C When you throw a dice twenty times you will get at least one 6.

D Christmas Day next year will be celebrated in December.

E Your Head Teacher will jump right over your school.

Certain	
Very Likely	
Even chance	
Not very likely	
Impossible	

Now make up five sentences, A to E, of your own so that one is certain,
one is very likely and so on. Illustrate each sentence by marking an arrow
on the probability line:

Impossible	Certain
0	1

Be careful – there is a difference between genuinely impossible
situations and those which are just extremely unlikely.

> **Links with the Classbook**
>
> **Unit 10**
> *pages* 66–68
>
> **Unit 20**
> *pages* 138–139

10.3 Fair or unfair?

Sometimes when you are playing games it appears that some people have an advantage over others and that the game is unfair.

Here are some games to play. You have to decide whether they are fair games, that is everyone has the same likelihood of winning, or unfair games, that is some people are more likely to win than others.

Rules

Each game is for 2, 3 or 4 players. Each player chooses one of the four quadrants (or quarters) of the 'board' and then they take turns in throwing the two dice.

If a player can make one of the numbers in their quadrant, then they can mark that square, otherwise the dice are passed to the next player. Each player has 10 turns.

The winner is the person who has made the most marks. (You can mark a square more than once provided it is on a different turn.)

Game 1

In this game you have to work out the difference between the numbers on the two dice.

2	4	3	2
5	1	1	0
0	1	0	5
3	5	4	6

Is the game fair? ....

Game 2

In this game you have to add up the numbers on the two dice.

8	6	11	3
5	7	5	6
12	1	10	7
3	10	3	9

Is the game fair? ....

Links with the Classbook
Unit 10 *pages 66–68*

10.4 Probability experiments

Winston wanted to know the probability of the weather being rainy near his home. He recorded the weather on 50 random days and recorded the results in a tally chart like this:

Rainy		13
Not rainy		37

Winston wrote this brief report in his notebook:

Impossible   Certain

0   1

For each of the probability questions below do an experiment.

Collect at least 50 results in a tally chart.

Present your conclusion in a brief report similar to Winston's.

You may decide the result is likely, has an even chance, or is unlikely.

1   You toss a coin and it lands as 'Heads'.

2   You throw a dice and get a 5.

3   You throw a drawing pin and it lands point up.

4   You throw two dice and the total score is a prime number.

5   You take a card from a pack and it is a picture card (Jack, Queen or King).

6   You toss a coin and throw a dice to obtain 'Tails' and a 6.

7   You throw two dice to obtain a product which is even.

Now make up some probability experiments of your own and try them out.

Links with the Classbook

Unit 10
pages 66–68

Unit 20
pages 138–139

10.5 The great duck race

Some towns have an annual duck race on the river when people can take bets on which duck will win the race. This is a variation on the same theme which you can play in the comfort of your own classroom. All you need are some counters and a pair of dice.

Rules

There are twelve ducks racing and they are numbered from 1 to 12. Twelve people choose which duck they will support and then the fun begins ...

The pair of dice are thrown and the scores added together. The duck with the corresponding number swims forward one square.

The game continues in this way until one of the ducks swims over the finishing line

Duck	1	2	3	4	5	6	7	8	9	10	11	12

Play the game several times and then decide whether some ducks have an advantage over other ducks.

Is the game fair? ....

Links with the Classbook

Unit 10
pages 66–68